Sadistic Love

Bridget Jones

Copyright © 2021 Bridget Jones

All rights reserved. No part of this publication may be reproduced, distributed, or transmitted in any form or by any means, including photocopying, recording, or other electronic or mechanical methods, without the prior written permission of the publisher, except in the case of brief quotations embodied in critical reviews and certain other noncommercial uses permitted by copyright law.

ISBN- 978-1-951300-28-9

Liberation's Publishing LLC
West Point - Mississippi

Sadistic Love

Bridget Jones

Table of Contents

The Devil's Lair 3

Love Neglection 4

Danger 5

Unappreciated Love 6

Demonic 8

Knowledge 9

WiFi 10

Broken 12

What Lies Beneath 14

Breathless 16

Stranger in the Night 17

The Beginning 21

Searching 24

Desires 26

A Stranger Is He 28

Live or Die 31

Powerful Attraction 32

Missing Him 34

Good vs Evil 36

I Can See Her Soul 38

Welcome to the dark side of love poems. Love can be a very tricky and sneaky little devil. It will have you entangled and trapped in its abyss of lies, hurt, and deceit. Just as I have been. One must always be careful, but not too careful. Welcome to my world.

The Devil's Lair

I danced on the devil's playground

I tapped danced in the fires of hell

I laughed as I lost myself in my feelings

I let him fuck my mind blindly

I let him partake of my soul

I let him manipulate my thoughts

I let him seduce me with his charm

And yet,

Again, and again,

I let his words caress my inner being

But I loved every moment of it

Until

I realized he had me whole heartedly

He had my spirit entwined with his

He could fuck me six ways from Sunday

And walk away and leave me stuck

Left trapped in this abyss called hell

Love Neglection

Love and Neglection is a drug. You become addicted with once it strikes you. You feel yourself slipping into this deep dark black hole. But the funny thing is that you don't even care. You don't even try to catch yourself allowing you to become consumed by it. Like an addict you keep telling yourself you'll get it together. I'll walk away eventually, but eventually never comes. What then? I'll tell you.

You increase the dosage to compensate for the empty feeling inside. You try hard to fill the void of neglection. When will eventually ever come? Will it come when it's too late? When you have lost it all. Either way love and neglect are a mind-boggling drug that consumes your every thought and leaves you trap.

Right now, I'm content with being trapped in my addiction. Will you live in the hellhole that is consuming you loving the neglect or neglecting… what loves you?

Trapped in love and neglect

Danger

I feel in love with danger.

The way you smell.

The way you taste.

The way you penetrate my soul from within,

But

When danger is no longer dangerous and has become safe what's left to love?

To love you and not to love you is torture in itself.

I crave the darkness within you, to release the beast that you try to keep hidden.

Give me what words cannot say to me.

Give me what I long for.

I feel in love with danger and I thought danger was you.

Unappreciated Love

You say you love me

You say you need me

You say I'm what you want

You say you can't see life without me,

But

You look straight pass me

You see the woman next to me

You see the woman behind me

A simple kiss from her

You like it

You want it

You need it

But a kiss from me

Passionate with fire from my soul you curse it

You deny it

You hate it

A touch from her melts you

You desire it

You love it

A touch from me bothers you

You dismiss it and walk away from it

I crave you

I want you

I need you

I love you

I adore you

I belong to you

But

You need her

You want her

You love her

You belong to her

And

I'm left looking for who belongs to me…

No one

I'm left unappreciated

Unwanted, unloved, looking, wanting, needing, searching

Until her love runs dry for you

Then it is I who still belongs to you

unappreciated

Demonic

The dark side awakening

That which is dead feed

My demon brings them back to life

How? You may ask

Walk with me to the dark side of love

I don't fuck

I make love

I make love to your mind while caressing your soul

I intwine in your temple

This kind of love is divine

Yet hard to find

I bind our spirits while we're locked eye to eye as lovers

I will take your soul to hell with mine

As we dance on the flames of burning desires

For the name unspoken is the key to my hidden pleasures

It sets my world on fire

You will forever be mine as one soul entwined

Until the end of time

Knowledge

I crave your thoughts

Your thoughts give me knowledge

Your knowledge is the key to unlock the subliminal thoughts of mine, that broaden our horizon

Without you I am nothing more than a winkle in time

The knowledge is what makes us shine

That is what makes me smile from within

Your knowledge

Bridget Jones

WiFi

I used to be your Wi-Fi.

You used and abused me daily.

But even when my connection was slow

I was always somehow there when you needed to connect.

But when you got tired of me running slow…
on somedays you ran out on me.

You replaced me with another Wi-Fi.

Sure, it was fast at first.

It was great until you found out it was only temporary Wi-Fi.

And when your new Wi-Fi ran out on you and you could no longer connect…

You returned to me

I should have disconnected and erased you from my device's memory

But…

I didn't.

WHY?

Because my Wi-Fi was unlimited,

Always there for you to connect to.

Ladies don't be a man's temporary Wi-Fi.

Be his only Wi-Fi, unlimited.

If not disconnect from all devices.

Who am I?

I am your Wi-Fi.

Broken

To have you and not have you is torture in itself.

I crave your touch.

I long for you,

To be next to you

To have you

To hold you

To be near you

The thought of losing you scares the hell out of me.

But to know that you'll always be here with me comforts me.

But to be alone breaks me

To have you and not have you is torture in itself.

To reach out to you in the darkest hour and find no one saddens my soul.

To cry out for you only to be met with dead silence opens the holes in my heart.

To want you, to need you

To desire you

Only to be turned away breaks me.

Sadistic Love

To have you and not have you is torture in itself.

To be with you is to be broken

And Baby… because of you, I am broken.

What Lies Beneath

Call me what you want…

But what I want is the darkness inside of you.

I want the danger that grows within you.

I want the beast to become unleashed.

I want your demon to roam free.

I want the terror that lurks in the dead of night.

I want your hands upon my throat…

Your tongue in my mouth

Your eyes piercing through my soul

Your shaft in the pit of my stomach.

I want the woman in me to tremble with fear from the sound of your voice.

I want you to make me submit and climax uncontrollably.

I want you to engulf my breast until the nectar in me trickles down my legs…

Leaving me breathless, panting for more.

Trace my body with your protruding manhood.

Set my soul on fire.

I want the darkness. The danger. The beast. The demons to play on the sole of my soul.

Make passionate love to my thoughts and manipulate my inner being.

Make my body burst into flames hotter than hell that would put Satan to bed.

Call me what you want…

But what I want is for you to unleash the beast that is in you inside me.

Breathless

Kiss me from your soul.

Touch me from your mind.

Make love to me from your heart.

Caress my thoughts with your stroke.

Let me drink the nectar from your neck.

Embody me with your hidden desires.

Ignite my fire, then quench me with that which flows from your body leaving me…Breathless

Stranger in the Night

As I'm walking down this dark street, I hear footsteps behind me.

I speed up my pace and the footsteps behind me follow.

I try to ignore it.

The fear is building up with in me, my mind is racing, my heart is pounding.

I want to look back, but fear stops me.

I cannot look, I keep walking faster and faster.

I turn the corner and the light of the streetlamp blows out.

It's dark.

I stop dead in my tracks panicking.

What do I do?

Do I turn and face the footstep?

Do I run away from the footsteps that are getting closer?

My heart starts pounding harder.

Yet I feel myself getting moist between my legs.

I try to shake it and run.

Just as I begin to run out of the shadows a hand grabs me.

He pulls me against him.

I try to scream, but his hand covers my mouth.

He throws me against the wall.

He rips my shirt open.

His mouth swallows my breast.

He pulls my skirt up and I stand there shaking with fear.

I cannot move as something inside of me wants more.

Something inside of me has me wanting this.

I try to fight back, but he controls me.

My eyes begin to change. Something inside of me breaks.

With His hands around my throat, I yearn for something more.

He tries to kiss me, but I turn away.

He grips my mouth and opens it.

I feel his tongue slip into my mouth.

It was then that I realized… I wanted this.

I was sucking his tongue deeper and deeper.

I push him away and run.

I want him to chase me.

He does.

He catches me, or maybe, I let him catch me.

He throws me to the ground and devours me.

His hardness penetrates my soul.

I feel a gush of fluids leave me.

He fucks me rough and hard,

But the pain is sheer pleasure.

I like it. I want it. I need it.

I beg him to stop while crying out, trying to hold back this intense fire that is building within me.

I can no longer hold it. I can no longer control myself.

I push back against his hardened shaft. I begin to fuck him back.

The hunted has become the hunter.

He is now my prey. I flip him over and mount him.

I realized he was awakening my demons.

I fuck him like a thief in the night.

His eyes begin to glow with shock as I ride him.

Something inside of me begins to change.

Something in me breaks loose.

As I climax on top of him bare breasted glistening from the moonlight.

A surge rushes electricity through me. It leaves me weakened and him stunned.

I gather myself and walk away, leaving him lying there wondering what just happened.

As reality hits,

I had just become the stranger in the night.

The Beginning

As I lay in my bed eyes filled with tears,

My mind is racing in a million directions.

Heartbroken.

Face saddened

I close my eyes

I see him use his keys to my heart and walked into my soul

I breath in deep and exhale softly

He whispers in my ear,

"Baby I'm sorry. All I want is you."

As he grabs hold of my mind and remove every layer of doubt.

He eases my thoughts.

He bends down and starts to kiss me in my most sensitive places

With the fire burning inside of me I bring myself to tell him to stop

He only kisses me more

He tells me, "Be quiet. Don't speak."

He raises up and slides his soul into mine.

As we become one, I brace myself.

My nails dig into his back.

As he goes deeper, so do my nails into his flesh

As he moans with pleasure, so do I.

I beg him to stop as he grabs hold of my hands locking his in mine, he raises them above my head.

He slides one hand down to my breast.

As he squeezes, I let out a cry.

He grabs hold of my neck.

As he squeezes it oh so soft yet firmly

I don't hold back.

He's all I want.

My breast disappears within his mouth.

The feeling between my legs consumes me.

As I beg for more and more, he goes deeper and deeper.

As we burst into flames, he asks me,

"Who am I?"

With a shaky voice and a whimper, I reply,

"Unspoken My King Is You."

He then replies,

"This was only the beginning."

Searching

As time passes, it brings about a change.

And baby you're changing.

As you change, so do we.

Where you once connected to my inner being you are no longer there leaving it empty.

Yet, I look for you, searching for more.

The desire of wanting you…

The thought of you tearing my clothes off

Filling my mouth with the taste of your tongue

The need for you to be inside of me

The passion of us rolling, bumping, grinding, moaning

The sweat dropping off of you

You touching my breast

The thought of you caressing my body so firm

Yet so soft.

The intensity of anticipation, waiting for you to break me open

Thrust your massive rock hardness into me

Sadistic Love

I can no longer wait to grab your back and pull you closer.

Between my thighs the desire of wanting you, needing you, consumes me in every way.

The way you rolled me over going deeper inside of me

My jaws dropping with excitement, gasping for air

Biting my pillow as I scream for you to go deeper

You pinning me in the bed and thrusting harder, harder, deeper, deeper.

The tighter you hold me down the wetter I get.

The hunger in me builds and in an instance pure ecstasy.

We unite as one intwined in each other's love.

But as time passes it brings about a change

And Baby you're changing

And now I'm left searching.

Desires

Mind racing body shaking

The visions I'm embracing

The dark urges I'm facing

Hearing the whispers of a man wanting you…

Followed by the smells of erotica as I move through the darkness

My hand feels the silky-smooth surface of a man's torso

To further examine I lean into him

I feel his breath upon my face

As I look up our lips touch

As I begin to move backwards

A mans hand grabs the nape of my back

My hands begin pacing the body of what appears to be a god up and down, down and up

As my hand lands on his protruding manhood, I jump and try to move.

He grabs me and places it on his massive hard cock.

He leans in and asks,

"Do as you please. I'm yours."

In that moment I don't know what came over me.

I find my knees bending, my mouth opening, my body shaking, mind racing as…

I suck him in. Tasting the sweet nectar that is within him.

I can feel his nature growing even bigger in my mouth.

Desire forms as I spread my legs.

I touch myself and feel the waters flowing dripping from me.

As I spread them further in that moment, I whisper,

"I want you inside of me. Fulfill my desire."

A Stranger Is He

I fell asleep on the couch in the middle of the night.

Someone broke in and took hold of me.

He pinned me down and starts to kiss me.

He moves to my neck.

I scream for him to let me go, but

To my surprise the more I resist him the more it turns him on.

He kisses my lips and I become aroused.

I French kiss him back and his hands between my legs stiffens me.

He pushes my pelvic into his.

I feel his erection against my wet nature.

I scream for him to stop, even though to my surprise I'm quiet turned on.

I want it bad.

Crazy huh.

A stranger has managed to arouse me like I've never been aroused before.

I want him so bad he grabs me by the throat.

He leans my head back giving him full access to my neck.

His teeth drop as he bites down hard opening up the gateway to hell.

He begins to pound into my soul.

His mouth fills with blood.

Long deep hard thrust makes me scream.

He caresses my mind with his every touch.

Every inch of my body is on fire.

He goes deeper and bite harder.

My cries become whimpers, whining, moans.

He asks me, "Do you dare have me to stop?"

Without answering him, I grab him, this stranger.

My spirit begins to cry out in pure erotic emotions.

I pull him closer and deeper and whisper,

"I have waited my entire life for you."

The thirst inside me builds as it burns to his touch.

As I try to shake lose and regain myself, he asks,

"Who am I"

"A stranger of pure pleasure." I responded as I climaxed.

He said, "No, I am a lifetime memory. Nothing more than a dream.

As the darkness became darker and the vision became faint, I realized the stranger was me.

It was nothing more than a dream.

Live or Die

Blinded by love.

I'd rather be abused and beaten than to be a victim of love.

Broken hearted wounds and bruises heal.

But a broken heart never does, because it is constantly being broken by love.

Some things can never be fixed.

Which would you choose?

To choose love is to die daily.

To choose pain is to heal with time.

But you yet live.

What's your choice?

To live or to die.

Powerful Attraction

How can this be?

The Passion.

The Electricity between the two of us is undeniable, uncontrollable.

His lips upon mine send chills down my spine.

His touch is oh so divine.

His voice so deep with thunder it makes my body quiver.

The sweet soft whispers make me shiver with excitement.

How can this be?

The Passion.

The Electricity between the two of us is uncontrollable, undeniable.

How can two people love each other so much,

But walk away with tears in their eyes

Hurt in their hearts.

The moments we shared seized and ripped from us as far as the day is from night.

How can this be?

For now, the taunting task of wiping the tears way.

One day I pray that this undeniable, uncontrollable electricity finds its way back to us.

Missing Him

Sitting here with visions of him imprinted on my mind,

Thoughts are running wild inside of me.

I can't stand these feelings.

The fear of losing him scared the hell out of me.

He's my king, my heart.

The passion in my eyes.

The fire in my soul

The air I breathe

He's the reason I smile from within

Just to feel his warm embrace around me

His breath upon my neck

His tongue next to mine

To feel him inside of me

To make love to my mind

To seduce my thoughts

I can't do without him.

The love I have for him is crazy

And Yet

I remain untouched or tainted by any other than his hands.

I'm missing him like crazy

Wanting him

Needing him

Craving him

Good vs Evil

Excuse me,

You're a beautiful black queen.

And I see in you what he does not see.

Give me a smile and I'll leave you.

Cause I see what he can't see.

You're broken, and I can fix that.

You're tired and I can help with that.

You're wanting real love, and I can give you that.

Just tell me where you'll be tomorrow.

And I won't say a word.

I just want to be near you.

Cause I see the queen in you that he does not see.

I see the strength in you, that he breaks daily.

But I will restrengthen that.

I see the pain he caused daily.

But I will heal that.

I see the strong black woman within you that he tares down because of his own insecurities.

That woman I will rebuild her.

I see the heart that bleeds through already stitched wounds

But if you give me a chance I will repair that.

Because I see the queen that is in you that he does not see.

Give me the chance and I will save you

Because I made you in an image of me.

I Can See Her Soul

I often see her cry and wonder, "Why?"

I see her soul about to die.

A tare here, a tare there

With a bowed head and I wondered, "Why?"

I can see her soul about to die.

With the prettiest smile the most radiant eyes,

The sweetest laugh and I wonder, "Why?"

I can see her soul bout to die.

Too much pain

Too much hurt

Tortured by memories

She cannot go on anymore.

And I wondered, "Why?"

I can see her soul about to die.

With a heart pierced with holes her thoughts wounded with a knife in her back. I wondered, "Why?"

And the memories of you left on the table where she last laid them.

Sadistic Love

I often see her cry

And wonder, "Why?"

But I can see her soul about to die.

With a heart now black, her smile upside down, and eyes cold as Ice

I can see her soul and it's about to die.

Rest easy Baby Girl eyes to the sky.

I've watched her soul lay down and die.

As I cry and say goodbye and wonder why?

Bridget Jones

Sadistic Love

September 10, 1972 – September 8, 2013

In Loving memory of my beloved sister Kontina Bonner

I love you more than life itself.

Rest Easy My Love

Bridget Jones

www.ingramcontent.com/pod-product-compliance
Lightning Source LLC
Chambersburg PA
CBHW062031120526
44592CB00037B/2204

What happens when love in all its purity is turned into a weapon? What happens when what sounds like love and feels like love is found out to be nothing but a screenplay with you playing the star role as prey.

See, we've all been caught up in "love." What you thought was just you and he, ended up being you he and she and God knows who else. But even in knowing, something inside of you wants to stay with the lie. You go into the dark places of your mind and create a place for this twisted love to exist. You make excuses for his abuses. You say it's your fault. You say He must love me because he touches me like he loves me. He says the right words. All the time the reality is that you have blinded your eyes to is always before you. You have become a part of a sadistic love affair. Call yours what you like. Sugar coat it if you must. But to come out of it you must see it for what it is. Then you must speak yourself out of the dark place you placed yourself in and come into the Light.